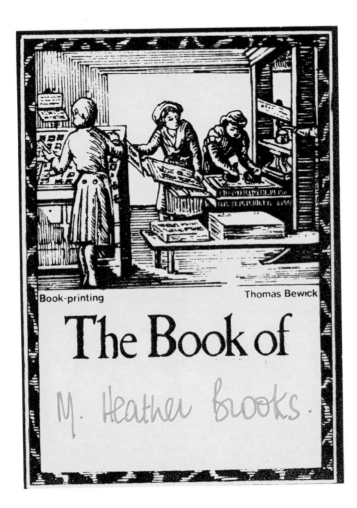

Book-printing   Thomas Bewick

The Book of

M. Heather Brooks.

Traditional

Lace Making

Sally Johanson

VNR VAN NOSTRAND REINHOLD COMPANY
New York Cincinnati Toronto London Melbourne

Van Nostrand Reinhold Company Regional Offices:
New York   Cincinnati   Chicago   Millbrae   Dallas

Van Nostrand Reinhold Company International Offices:
London   Toronto   Melbourne

This book was originally published in Sweden
under the title *Knyppling*
by LTs Förlag, in collaboration with the
Swedish Lace-Making Association

Copyright © for *Knyppling*
by Sally Johanson 1964
English copyright © Van Nostrand Reinhold Company Ltd. 1974

Translated from the Swedish by E. and T. W. Summers

Library of Congress Catalog Card Number: 73-16709
ISBN: 0 442 30037 9

This book is filmset in Optima,
printed by Jolly and Barber Ltd., Rugby,
and bound by the Ferndale Book Company, South Wales

Published by Van Nostrand Reinhold Company Inc.,
450 West 33rd Street, New York N.Y. 10001 and
Van Nostrand Reinhold Company Ltd.,
25–28 Buckingham Gate, London SW1E 6LQ

16   15   14   13   12   11   10   9   8   7   6   5   4   3   2   1

Library of Congress Cataloging in Publication Data

Johanson, Sally.
   Traditional lace making.

   Translation of Knyppling.
   1.   Bobbin lace.   I.   Title.
TT805.J6313   746.2'2   73-16709
ISBN 0-442-30037-9

Contents

Fig. I–1. The King's lace. The original garment in silver or gold was owned by Gustav Adolf II of Sweden. The Royal Armoury, Stockholm. Bridal crown made from gold thread.

Introduction

Lace first began to be used decoratively during the 16th and 17th centuries, not only on dress, but on both bed and table linen as well. In the Middle Ages, improved textile techniques arising from the invention of the spinning wheel and the hand loom further encouraged higher standards of clothing. Flax cultivation and linen production were increased in order to meet the growing demand for improved comfort, hygiene, and appearance. Linen soon became a necessity among the upper classes, but did not expand into more general use until the end of the Middle Ages, remaining a luxury until the beginning of the 19th century, when a much cheaper competitor, cotton, entered the market. The possession of linen clothing began to be fashionable in the Middle Ages when suitable trimmings were expected to be displayed on outer garments, and continued into the Renaissance and Baroque periods. Collars and cuffs on men's and women's clothing remained one of the most cherished decorative elements from the end of the 15th century until well into the 18th. The popularity of lace was at its peak during this period, as it was a natural and predominant accompaniment to linen.

Out of the demand for such finery different techniques developed, of which the sewn and bobbin-made laces were the most prominent. The technique of working lace with bobbins, which already existed in the Middle Ages, rapidly evolved during the second half of the 15th century, as a result of being adopted by fashion. Improvements probably took place about this time in the tools of the craft – pillows, bobbins, pins, and pricked patterns. Two distinctive lace-making techniques can, generally speaking, be recognized: the traditional method, which works on a cushion-like pillow, using either no 'pins' at the edge or only a few shaped from wood, and a more advanced one, which employs the pricked pattern typical of finely worked lace.

This book is intended to provide elementary instruction in one version of the latter type of lace-making, which was originally developed in Vadstena, Sweden.

Fig. 1–2. St Lars lace. Early 18th century design, the original in gold thread. St Lars Church, Linköping.

1. Tools and materials

The lace-maker, like other craftsmen and women, needs good tools to achieve good results. The tools discussed below apply principally to bobbin-made lace.

Pillows

Most pillows are oval (Fig. 1–1), and, although the padding must be firm, the overall effect must not be too high for working in comfort. A suitable pillow size is about 18½ × 22½ in. (470 × 570 mm.). The covering should be of a smooth material, preferably in a single colour. The detachable roller must be very tightly packed, otherwise it soon becomes too springy and incapable of supporting the pins. A wedge, or in some cases a catch, holds the roller firmly to the pillow.

Handles should be attached to the pillow to make it portable. A narrow cotton band is essential for keeping the bobbins in their proper order. This can be done in a number of ways, for instance, by pegging the cotton band at intervals between pairs (Fig. 1–2), or by using a double band, which is twisted after passing each bobbin (Fig. 1–3). The band must be fastened at both ends. An alternative method is to fasten the bobbins with press studs, using double cotton bands supplied with their own studs.

It is useful to have an extra piece of cotton or a towel at the front of the pillow, in order to protect its surface against wear from the bobbins. Another piece of soft material (such as flannel) should be fitted round the roller when making wider laces. (See p. 9.) Always keep a dust cover of cotton or ticking with the pillow.

The pillow should stand on a table at a convenient height, about 2 ft. (620 mm.); exact measurements depend on the overall height of the pillow when on the table. The most common pillow, as illustrated, is 5 in. (120 mm.) high.

A variation on the pillow described above replaces the roller by a revolving pillow. This is usually used for making small round edgings. The new Christina pillow improves on the traditional design further with a revolving outer disk. (See Fig. 3–1, p. 43.) Here also, the roller can be exchanged for another inset pillow.

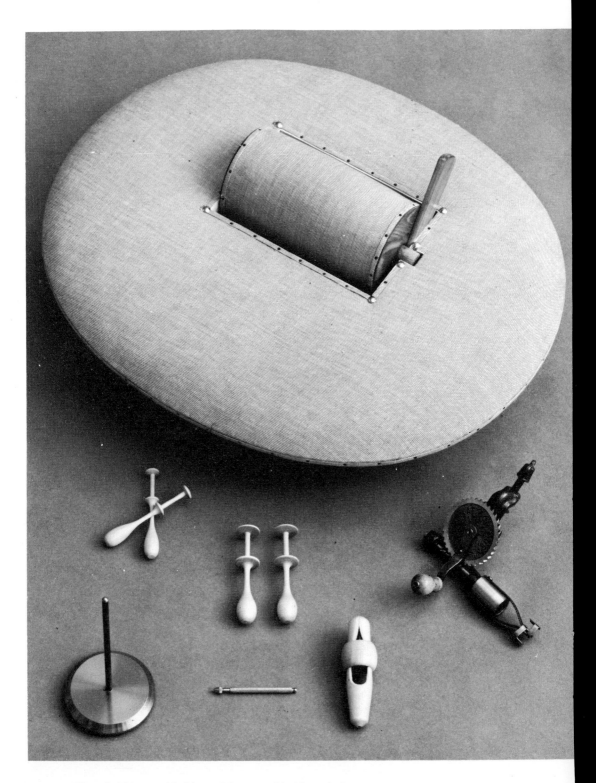

Fig. 1–1. Pillow, bobbins, reel holder, pricker, spool holder, winder.

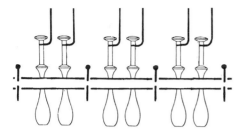

Fig. 1–2. Bobbins fastened
to pillow with cotton band.

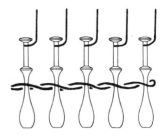

Fig. 1–3. Bobbins fastened
to pillow with double band.

Bobbins

The most commonly used bobbins are made from birchwood, either 4 in.
(100 mm.) in length for lace thread, or 4¼ in. (105 mm.) for coarser thread.
(See Fig. 1–1.) The bobbins will last longer if they are first dipped in boiled
linseed oil a couple of times, then left to dry for a good month before use.

Pins

With work that requires only a coarse thread, use pins with a small glass
head or steel pins. For lace woven with fine thread, thin steel pins are
best. Work is easier with flexible pins of good quality; coarse pins will
wear out the pattern more quickly.

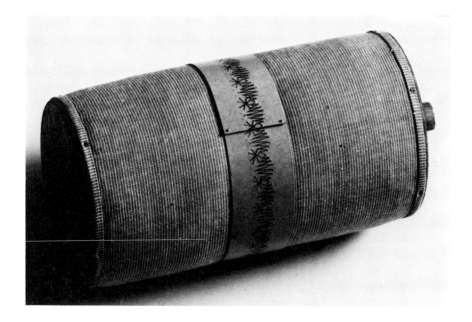

Fig. 1–4. Roller with pattern attached.

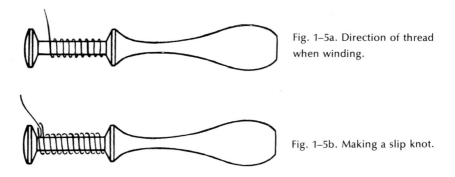

Fig. 1–5a. Direction of thread when winding.

Fig. 1–5b. Making a slip knot.

Pricking

Bobbin-worked lace requires pricked patterns. When copying a lace, first pencil the pattern on to graph paper (usually printed in millimetres). Each pinhole marks a step in the work (see Figs. 2–9 and 2–34), and demands great accuracy. Distances between pinholes must reflect exactly the progress of the original; any deviation would fault the copy lace. For fine lace, particularly lace with a tulle net ground, the pattern has to be followed very carefully, remembering that the pin distances lengthwise will be shorter than they are across. (See Fig. 2–44.)

Pin the completed pattern firmly to the lace board (pricking card). Hold the pricker (Fig. 1–1), allowing only the point to enter the card (a precaution that will reduce unevenness in the finished product). After pricking, use Indian ink to draw in the line work. Remember, a well-worn pattern with enlarged holes will not produce good lace.

The pricking procedure described above is time-consuming, and it is not recommended for beginners. A great variety of already pricked patterns are now available commercially through the usual retailers and handicraft societies.

Thread

Good quality linen should be used. English linen is available in a variety of thicknesses and gradations of bleaching.

Mark the pattern with the quality of thread recommended for a particular lace. This will depend primarily on the spacing of the pricking, and on other factors such as the composition, the structure, and, to some extent, the intended use of the lace. As a general rule, a lace is designed to suit a particular thread; it would not look as beautiful if executed differently.

Winding the bobbins

Threads should be wound evenly along the spool. First, tie a loop round the bobbin and tighten it; then wind the thread either by hand or with a winder. The direction of the thread is illustrated in Fig. 1–5a. In winding by hand, the bobbin should rotate so that the thread is distributed evenly and tightly along the length of the spool. Threads should never be wound carelessly.

Naturally, a mechanical device will give better results. There are special winders for lace-making, as in Fig. 1–1, as well as spool holders for use on a weaver's winder. (See Fig. 1–1.)

After winding, secure the thread with a loop. (See Fig. 1–5b.) This must be carried out correctly, since the loop serves a double purpose – to prevent the thread from unwinding and at the same time to control the running of the thread.

A reel holder is useful for storing wound thread. (See Fig. 1–1.)

Preparations before starting

Lay the pattern on the roller so that the border of the lace will come out on the right. At the seam, the pattern should overlap about ¾ in. (20 mm.) toward the worker. (See Fig. 1–4.) The pattern, of course, must fit perfectly so that the design is not broken.

The actual process of lace-making may be started in a number of ways. First of all, the required number of bobbins must be evenly distributed, either in groups across the pattern, or (where a row of holes follows throughout the graph) with three pairs to each pin at the foot, and two pairs to each pin across the pattern. A later chapter explains how to start different types of laces. The position of the worker's hands is shown in Fig. 3–1 on p. 43.

When a thin thread breaks in the course of the work, use a reef or a weaver's knot. If the break occurs just beside a pin, or when a coarse thread is worked, undo a short length of lace up to the nearest pin, make a loop and hang it on the pin, then weave it in with the rest. Use a needle to fit inconspicuously into the pattern. To make a join of coarse threads or a gimp, bring in a fresh bobbin of similar thread and weave both threads together far enough to secure the new thread firmly. Lay the old thread aside, to be eventually cut off.

Fig. 1–6. 6–9 year olds attending a class.

2. First steps

Lace is made by varying the two basic movements, cross and twist, which interlock the threads. (See Figs. 2–2 and 2–3.) Certain combinations of these movements have become standard stitches and grounds. The threads are moved by bobbins, which are always worked in pairs.

The general rule in foundation work is that the pair entering the ground from the footside receives the number of twists applicable to that ground. The same rule applies to the number of twists worked with the pair travelling to and from the cloth and net ground.

To learn the basic rules of lace-making, first work through Patterns 1 to 8 in numerical order including Sampler I. (Pattern 3 may be omitted.) The numbers referred to in the pattern instructions correspond to particular steps in the appropriate diagrams.

Fig. 2–1. Starting position.

Fig. 2–2. Crossing.

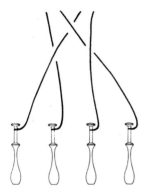

Fig. 2–3. Twist, from right to left.
Cross and twist to make a half-stitch.

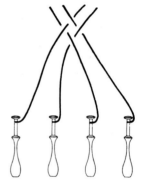

Fig. 2–4. Cross, twist, and cross
to make a whole stitch.

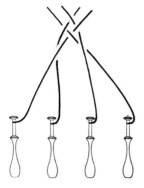

Fig. 2–5. Cross, twist, cross and twist
to make a whole stitch and twist.

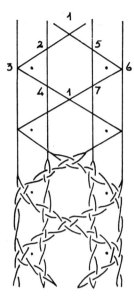

Fig. 2–6. Diagram for
'Head and foot'
insertion lace.

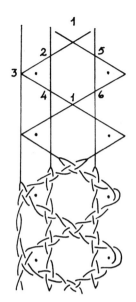

Fig. 2–7. Diagram for
'Head and foot'.

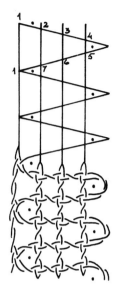

Fig. 2–8. Diagram for
'Steps'.

Pattern 1. 'Head and foot' insertion lace

Material: English linen No. 50/3 or 40/2, 6 pairs of bobbins.

Work this lace with whole stitch and twist, 1,2,3, pin-up, 4,5,6, pin-up, 7, and repeat from 1. (See Fig. 2–6.) To produce a firm footside, give an extra twist to the edge pair after stitches 3 and 6.

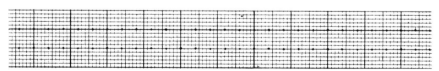

Fig. 2–9. Pattern for 'Head and foot' insertion lace.

Fig. 2–10. 'Head and foot' insertion lace.

Pattern 2. 'Head and foot'

Material: English linen No. 50/3 or 40/2, 5 pairs of bobbins.

Work this lace with whole stitch and twist, 1,2,3, pin-up, 4,5, pin-up, 6, and repeat from 1. (See Fig. 2–7.)

As in the previous example, give an extra twist to the edge pair after stitch 3. Also give an extra twist to the pair after 5, which encloses the pin, to make a firmer and more definite head.

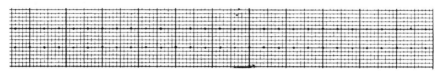

Fig. 2–11. Pattern for 'Head and foot'.

Fig. 2–12. 'Head and foot'.

Pattern 3. 'Steps'

Material: English linen No. 50/2, 5 pairs of bobbins.

Work this lace with whole stitch and twist, 1, pin-up, 2,3,4, pin-up, 5,6,7, and repeat from 1. (See Fig. 2–8.) Give an extra twist to the edge pair after stitch 1, and to the pair after 4 which encloses the pin in the head.

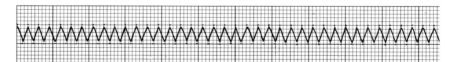

Fig. 2–13. Pattern for 'Steps'.

Fig. 2–14. 'Steps'.

Pattern 4. 'Wood anemone'

Material: English linen No. 50/2, 12 pairs of bobbins.

This lace consists of clothwork with whole stitch and twist worked on the footside. Work the cloth with whole stitch. (See Fig. 2–4.) The two bobbins which move across according to the pattern are referred to as the workers. When increasing the cloth add more bobbins. (See Fig. 2–17.) At 2,4, and 6, add new pairs of bobbins, to be joined by whole stitch to the workers. When decreasing width, leave out a pair at 6,8,10, (See Fig. 2–17), and bring them back into operation as the width increases, at 21,22,24. (See Fig. 2–17.)

When putting up a pin in the cloth, twist the workers once.

Start this lace by working whole stitch and twist. Put up pin 1 between the second and third pair on the left side of the lace. Now, the second pair of bobbins becomes the workers; follow the pattern, passing through two pairs with a whole stitch before a twist. Put up pin 2. Take the workers back, working a whole stitch through two pairs; twist and join to the foot pair by whole stitch and twist. Put up pin 3. Continue working in this way up to and including pin 10. Work the right side of the lace (pins 11–20) in the same way. Twist each pair twice from pins 6,8, and 10 and from 16,18, and 20 before the central cloth (pins 21–28) is worked. (See Fig. 2–17.) This completes one section of the pattern; return to pin 1 and repeat. Note that the bobbin pairs from pins 24–28 are each twisted twice.

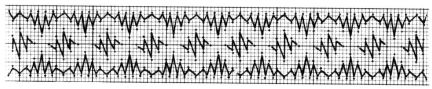

Fig. 2–15. Pattern for 'Wood anemone'.

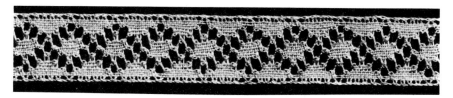

Fig. 2–16. 'Wood anemone'.

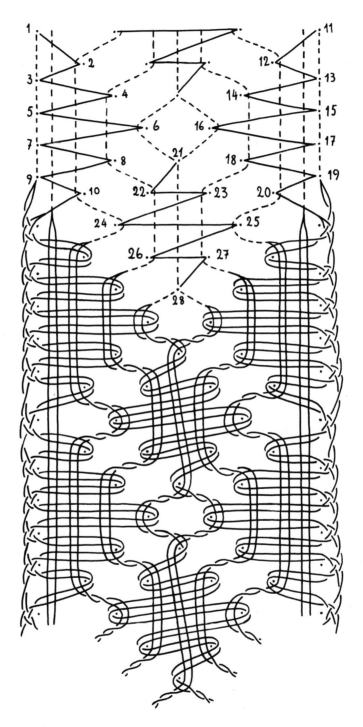

Fig. 2–17. Diagram for 'Wood anemone'.

Pattern 5. 'Sugar loaf with spider'

Material: English linen No. 90/2, 10 pairs of bobbins.

This lace consists of clothwork with an open head and a spider. Work with whole stitch and whole stitch and twist. (See Fig. 2–20.) Twist the bobbins twice from 8, before joining them to the footside by whole stitch and twist at 15. Join them at 16 and 20 by whole stitch and twist, pin-up, then whole stitch and twist. Note that the pairs, from the cloth and the footside, moving from 16 to 20, are each twisted twice.

Form an open head in the cloth by twisting the workers twice, moving from cloth to head. The sequence is: whole stitch and twist, twist workers, pin-up, whole stitch and twist. Give the workers an extra twist when moving from the head to the cloth, in order to maintain the same number of twists throughout the open head.

Work cloth as in Fig. 2–20, 1–14.

Work the spider in whole stitch in the order shown in Fig. 2–21, i.e. 1–4, pin-up, 5–8. Twist each pair three times before 1 and after 8 to form the 'spider's legs'.

Fig. 2–18. Pattern for 'Sugar loaf with spider'.

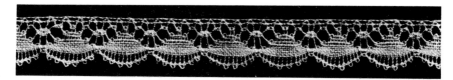

Fig. 2–19. 'Sugar loaf with spider'.

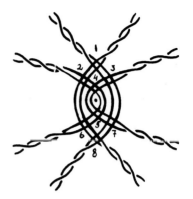

Fig. 2–21. Diagram for spider.

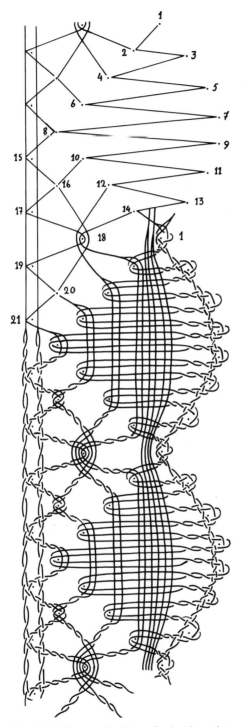

Fig. 2–20. Diagram for 'Sugar loaf with spider'.

Pattern 6. 'Waves'

Material: English linen No. 90/2, 11 pairs of bobbins.

This lace consists of Dieppe ground, half-stitch diamond, and clothwork.
(See Fig. 2–24.)

Work Dieppe ground by half-stitch, pin-up, half-stitch, twist.

Work half-stitch diamond by half-stitching in the direction shown in the
pattern. No additional twist is needed before putting up the pins.

The clothwork is described in Pattern 4. When this is used for the head,
it is better to twist the workers twice when closing round the pin at the
head.

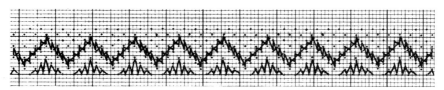

Fig. 2–22. Pattern for 'Waves'.

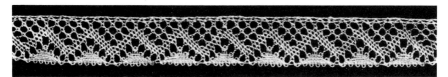

Fig. 2–23. 'Waves'.

Begin with the footside closest to the Dieppe ground. Work the foot in
the same manner as in the 'head and foot' pattern, i.e. join the second
and third pairs by whole stitch and twist, join the first and second pairs by
whole stitch and twist, pin-up between second and third pairs already
joined by whole stitch and twist. Give an extra twist to the extreme left
pair as well as to the third pair, i.e. the pair entering the Dieppe ground.
Work stitches according to Fig. 2–24, 1–10.

Start the half-stitch diamond at 11 (see Fig. 2–24), by joining the 7th and
8th pairs from the left, using half-stitch, then pin-up. Work three half-
stitches moving the bobbins pair by pair to 12, following the pattern.
Continue with half-stitch from 12 up to and including 21. The procedure
for increasing or decreasing the width is similar to that for the clothwork:
to increase, take in a fresh pair of bobbins at each pin-up (13,15,17,19);
to decrease, leave out a pair at each pin-up (12,14,16,18). Learn this

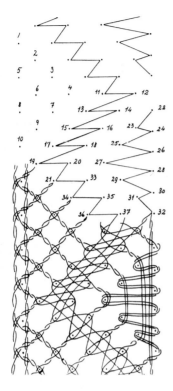

Fig. 2–24. Diagram for 'Waves'.

half-stitch diamond another way by practising the lace called 'Wedges'. (See p. 49.) Twist each pair of bobbins once, the half-stitch diamond entering from ground, at 12,14,16,18. Give them another twist before they join the cloth at the head (22 up to and including 32). Note that pairs entering from the cloth must be twisted twice at 27,29,31,32, before they are joined to the half-stitch diamond ground. Similarly, pairs entering from 19,21,34,36, should be twisted once. Repeat the entire pattern from 1.

Pattern 7. 'Peekaboo'

Material: English linen No. 50/2, 13 pairs of bobbins, English linen No. 18/5, one pair of bobbins.

This lace may also serve as an insertion lace, in which case an additional pair of bobbins will be required.

The lace consists of Dieppe ground, Brabant ground, clothwork, and gimp. (See Fig. 2–27.)

Work both the head and the foot with two pairs of bobbins, through which the workers pass with a whole stitch. Twist the workers twice when enclosing the pin at the head. At the foot, twist the workers once before they join the foot pair by whole stitch and twist. Give an extra twist to the edge pair in the foot.

Dieppe ground is described in Pattern 6.

Brabant ground is worked by half-stitch, pin-up, half-stitch, and twist as shown in Fig. 2–28.

The clothwork is described in Pattern 4.

Insert the gimp according to the pattern. When carrying this out with a Dieppe ground, work as shown in Fig. 2–29, i.e. lift the bobbins (of the pair) lying to the left, insert the gimp between the threads, and work a twist. (See Fig. 2–29.) To practise the Brabant ground and insertion of the gimp, work the lace called 'I spy' on p. 56.

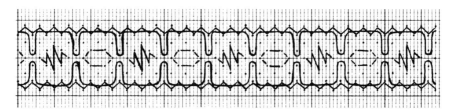

Fig. 2–25. Pattern for 'Peekaboo'.

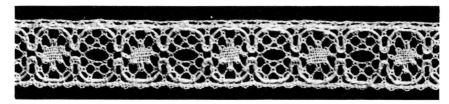

Fig. 2–26. 'Peekaboo'.

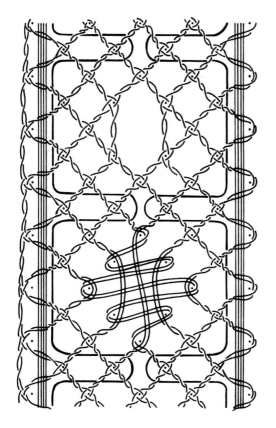

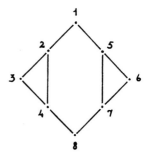

Fig. 2–28. Brabant ground.

Fig. 2–27. 'Peekaboo' includes Dieppe ground, Brabant ground, clothwork, and insertion of gimp.

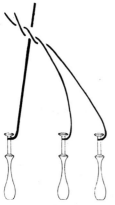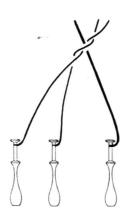

Fig. 2–29. Insertion of gimp.

Pattern 8. 'Plaited lace'

Material: English linen No. 50/3, 14 pairs of bobbins.

This lace consists of clothwork and plaits. (See Fig. 2–32.)

The clothwork is described in Pattern 4.

The plaits are formed by working a series of half-stitches, which are stretched tight after each movement. This stretching is essential to achieve an even lace. To join any two plaits, work a whole stitch, treating each pair as a single bobbin (cross, twist, pin-up, cross), as shown in Fig. 2–33. The workers should pass the plait after crossing so that the plait merges smoothly with the cloth.

The most common, traditional bobbin lace grounds are torchon, Dieppe, pinhole ground, tulle, whole stitch ground, Brabant, rose, cane, cloth, and half-stitch diamond.

To practise these grounds, learn Samplers I and II. Sampler I (grouped as Pattern 9), is intended for beginners, and the threads most suited to these grounds are No. 20/3–120/2. The grounds in Sampler II are more suited to thread No. 150/2 and others of finer quality. These samplers, of course, are intended only to familiarise the beginner with the various grounds; they are by no means definitive.

Start these laces, as well as any measured borders, by working a solid end using the same stitches and grounds that are used in the laces. Wind a fair amount of thread on a bobbin, and transfer part of it on to a second bobbin, leaving the pair connected.

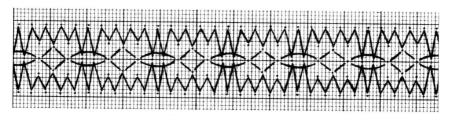

Fig. 2–30. Pattern for 'Plaited lace'.

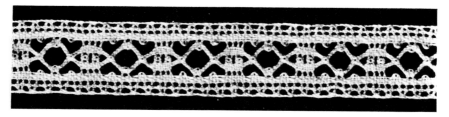

Fig. 2–31. 'Plaited lace'.

Fig. 2–32. Diagram for 'Plaited lace'.

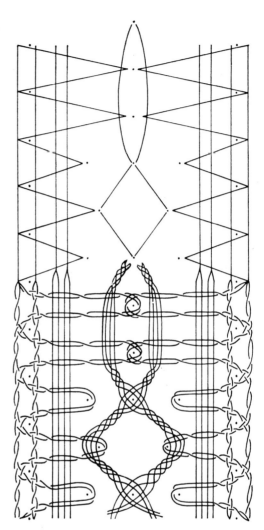

Fig. 2–33. 'Windmill' effect formed by two interlocking plaits.

Sampler I

Material: English linen No. 60/2, 14 pairs of bobbins, English linen No. 18/5, one pair of bobbins. Allow about 5 ft. (1·5 m.) of linen per bobbin.

Hang two pairs of bobbins over 1,2, and 11 (Fig. 2–36), and one pair over 3–10. Join the two pairs at 1 with a whole stitch, twisting the right-hand pair twice. Cover the pin according to the following method: (a) raise the pin, (b) push the stitch from in front to beyond the pinhole, and (c) replace the pin in the same hole. Beginners may find this series of movements helpful in performing the sequence: insert a temporary pin beyond the pattern pin, remove the pattern pin, make the stitch, insert the pattern pin to take the stitch, and remove the temporary pin (thus the stitch can be said to 'cover the pin'). Work a whole stitch, bringing in an extra pair of bobbins. Twist the workers twice. Work a half-stitch with the workers and the pair from 2. Cover the pin. Twist the pair going to the passives in the head. Give an extra twist to the pair continuing to 3, before taking in the next pair with half-stitch; pin-up, half-stitch and twist. Work the same sequence at 3 and 4. At 5, work a whole stitch with the pair from 1 and the new pair. Cover the pin. Twist the right-hand pair, now the workers, once. Cover the pin with a whole stitch. Repeat this procedure at 6. Twist the workers once in the usual way, before pinning-up. Work through the passives according to the pattern.

At 8, join the pairs with half-stitch, pin-up, half-stitch. Work the net ground in the usual manner, taking in the necessary new pairs at 9 and 10. Give an extra twist to the pair which goes into the foot from the stitch after 10. Work the foot in whole stitch and twist. Divide the two foot pairs, so that one bobbin from each pair is joined to the pair from 10. (Otherwise the outermost pair would become unstuck and would have to be hung again on the same pin.) Join the second and third pairs with a whole stitch and twist, then the first and second pairs, then cover the pin. Join the second and third pairs again with a whole stitch and twist. Give an extra twist to the pair on the extreme left, and to the third pair entering the ground.

In Sampler I, unless instructed otherwise, use a Dieppe ground. Work the sampler in accordance with the prickings on p. 28, as indicated below:
1. *Dieppe ground.* See Pattern 6 and Fig. 6–39.
2. *Clothwork.* See Pattern 4 and Fig. 2–36.
3. *Net ground.* See Pattern 6 and Fig. 2–36.
4. *Tallies* are worked with two pairs of bobbins. Hold tight or fasten three threads while taking the fourth over and under every other thread as shown in Fig. 2–37. When a closely-woven square is complete, twist the

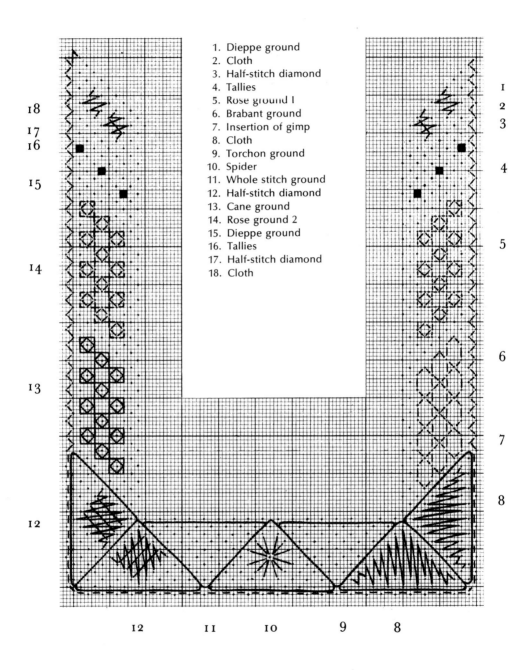

1. Dieppe ground
2. Cloth
3. Half-stitch diamond
4. Tallies
5. Rose ground 1
6. Brabant ground
7. Insertion of gimp
8. Cloth
9. Torchon ground
10. Spider
11. Whole stitch ground
12. Half-stitch diamond
13. Cane ground
14. Rose ground 2
15. Dieppe ground
16. Tallies
17. Half-stitch diamond
18. Cloth

Fig. 2–34. Pattern for Sampler I.

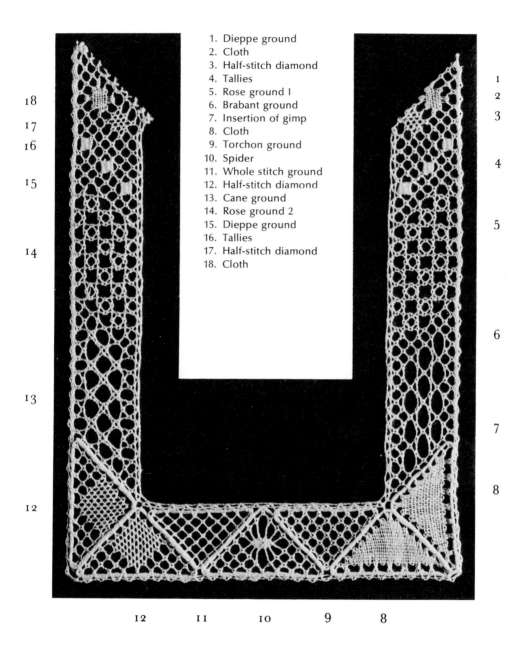

1. Dieppe ground
2. Cloth
3. Half-stitch diamond
4. Tallies
5. Rose ground 1
6. Brabant ground
7. Insertion of gimp
8. Cloth
9. Torchon ground
10. Spider
11. Whole stitch ground
12. Half-stitch diamond
13. Cane ground
14. Rose ground 2
15. Dieppe ground
16. Tallies
17. Half-stitch diamond
18. Cloth

Fig. 2–35. Sampler I.

Fig. 2–36a. Left-hand corner of Sampler I.   Fig. 2–36b. Left side of Sampler I.

Fig. 2–36c. Hanging bobbins for Sampler I.   Fig. 2–36d. Right-hand corner of Sampler I.

left-hand pair once. If necessary, hang this weaver in a loop round the outermost bobbin to the right. Another method is to work, immediately, first the left, then the right-hand pair of the adjoining ground, as shown in Fig. 2–38.

5. *Rose ground 1.* (See Fig. 6–45.) Half-stitch, pin-up, half-stitch, twist, as in Fig. 2–39. Note that in this pattern the last two pins of each section become the first two of the next.

6. *Brabant ground.* See Pattern 7 and Figs. 2–28 and 6–43.

7. *Insertion of gimp.* See Pattern 7 and Fig. 2–36. When two gimps change place, lay the right-hand thread over the left. In working the sampler, when two gimps lie side by side, do not twist the pairs holding them until both gimps have passed through. (See Figs. 2–36 and 6–32.)

Introducing a gimp leads to changes in working the head. The second pair of bobbins, now on the right, must be placed between the same pairs as the gimp in the head. Outside the gimp, work the head with whole stitch and twist, twist the workers, pin-up, and whole stitch and twist. After taking out the gimp, absorb this same pair into the headside, as in Fig. 2–36a.

8. *Clothwork.* (See Fig. 2–36d.) On every other row the cloth meets the working pair of bobbins from the outer edge. After finishing the net work, give each pair on the edge a single twist. Insert the gimps, one from each side, into the same pairs. When you have completed the diagonal marking the corner, lift the whole pattern together with its attached lace and pins, and rotate it through a quarter turn, then pin it back once more on to the roller. Put up a pin between the pairs of the plait in the corner hole and continue as before.

9. *Torchon.* This is worked in half-stitch, pin-up, and half-stitch as in Fig. 6–38.

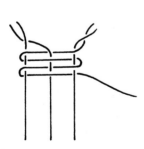

Fig. 2–37. Working a tally.

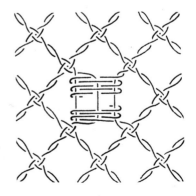

Fig. 2–38. Tally.

10. *Spider.* (See Pattern 5.) This is worked with 6 pairs of bobbins. Fig. 2–40 will show you how to join them.

11. *Whole stitch ground.* (See Fig. 6–42.)The method for this is: whole stitch and twist, pin-up.

12. *Half-stitch diamond ground.* (See Fig. 2–36.) When preparing to discontinue the gimps, work the gimp threads in the reverse direction between the same pairs of bobbins. Cut the threads as soon as they are secure enough.

13. *Cane ground.* (See Fig. 6–48.) This is worked in whole stitch and twist, as shown in Fig. 2–41, i.e. 1–5, whole stitch and twist; pin-up; 6–8, whole stitch and twist. Note that the last two stitches in one section become the first two in the following section.

14. *Rose ground 2.* (See Fig. 6–46.) Stitches are worked in the order shown in Fig. 2–42. Work 1 and 2 in whole stitch and twist; 3,4,5, and 6 with half-stitch, pin-up, half-stitch and twist; then 7 and 8 in whole stitch and twist.

15. *Dieppe ground.* See above.

16. *Tallies.* See above.

17. *Half-stitch diamond ground.* See above.

18. *Clothwork.* See above.

Finish the sampler along a row of pins round the corner, working the same stitch as in the lace. Then tie each pair of bobbins together with a reef knot and cut the threads off close to the knot.

Fig. 6–5 shows how to work the corner passives in the head.

The above details for starting and finishing a sampler are equally applicable to edgings.

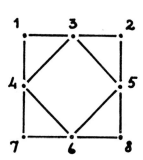

Fig. 2–39. Rose ground 1.

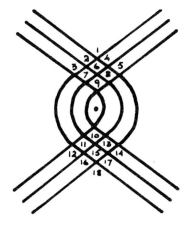

Fig. 2–40. Diagram for working the spider.

Sampler II

Material: English linen No. 160/2, 19 pairs of bobbins, LC No. 25, 3 bobbins. Allow about 6 ft (1·8 m.) of linen per bobbin.

Use graph paper for Sampler II, marked at 2·5–3 mm. (approximately ⅛ in. square). Draw in the corner at a right angle. Because of the displacement described on p. 10, the corner has to be built up and additional pairs of bobbins brought in. (See Fig. 2–45.)

Set out two pairs of bobbins at 1–5, and three pairs at 6, as shown in Fig. 2–45a. Start by inserting a gimp, giving a twist to each pair through which the gimp passes, from 2 up to and including 5. Join the two pairs at 2 with a half-stitch and an extra twist, cover the pin, then half-stitch and twist. Repeat this procedure at 3,4, and 5, as dictated by the pattern, with the gimps continuing towards the head. Be careful to twist each side of the gimps. Work the foot at 6, i.e. divide the bobbins so that one from each pair forms the first and second pairs from the left. (See Sampler I, p. 27). Similarly, join the second and third pairs by whole stitch and twist, repeating for the first and second pairs. Cover the pin. Work whole stitch and twist to join the second and third pairs, and give an extra twist to the outermost pair at the foot. Join the two pairs at 1 with whole stitch, give two twists to the workers on the right, cover the pin, then join the two pairs with whole stitch. Pass the new workers with whole stitch through two new pairs of bobbins temporarily brought in at 7, and continue with the workers through one of the pairs from 2. (See Fig. 2–45a.) When pinning-up, twist the workers once at the inside edge, and twice at the outer edge.

When working Sampler II, always join different grounds by working a pinhole ground unless otherwise instructed. Work the sampler by following the directions below and the pattern on p. 36.

1. *Pinhole ground.* (See Fig. 6–40.) The method for this is: half-stitch, twist, pin-up, half-stitch and twist. When working the outermost row of the footside, omit the extra twist to the left side of the stitch before pinning-up. This will eliminate tension on the pin, which could enlarge the hole. The same applies when working the head, i.e. omit the twist to the right side. (See Fig. 2–45.)

2. *Brabant ground.* (See Fig. 6–44.) This is worked by half-stitch, twist, pin-up, half-stitch, and twist. Follow the order as shown in Fig. 2–28.

3. *Rose ground.* (See Fig. 6–47.) This is worked by half-stitch, twist, pin-up, half-stitch, and twist. Follow the order as shown in Fig. 2–39.

4. *Clothwork and Brabant.* See above. The gimp passes between the workers of the cloth when the latter join the headside. Twist the workers once before pinning-up in the second row, i.e. before the workers from the two grounds meet. Thus these workers should each be twisted once. From ground 4 onwards, work half-stitch, twist left-hand pair, pin-up, and half-stitch, in order to join up with the head and the second row.

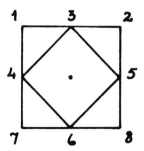

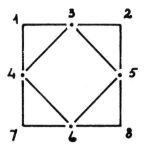

Fig. 2–41. Cane ground.   Fig. 2–42. Rose ground 2.

5. *Cane ground.* (See Fig. 6–48.) This is worked in whole stitch and twist as explained in Fig. 2–41.

6. *Tulle ground.* (See Fig. 6–41.) This is worked with half-stitch, two extra twists, then pin-up. The pairs are not joined after pinning-up. Start working the ground by adding an extra pair of bobbins at the foot. From now on these pairs, travelling to and from the foot, will pass two other pairs after each whole stitch. Work an extra twist before joining them, both at the foot and in the tulle ground. When pinning-up the cloth, place the pins at the side, and not, as usual, under the stitch. (See Figs. 2–45b and 6–4.)

7. *Clothwork with extra bobbins inserted and taken out.* (See Fig. 2–45b.) Add an extra pair of bobbins, hanging them on the gimp, then twist and work them into the cloth as with the other pairs. (See Fig. 2–45b.) When entering the cloth, the gimp passes without a twist either before or after. Remember to work the gimp in the reverse direction to the threads, as shown in Fig. 6–11. Take out the extra pair of bobbins when the cloth is completed. Tie a half-reef knot, laying the threads close to the gimp, one in each direction.

8. *Pointed head.* Add an extra pair of bobbins for the head when transferring from the cloth. To increase the width of the lace, join the first and second pairs at the head by whole stitch, twisting the outermost pair twice; then pin-up between these pairs, and work a whole stitch with the outermost pair toward the pinhole ground, thus passing the gimp. Twist before and after the gimp, work a twist, then continue with the pinhole ground.

On the inside of the clothwork, between the marked pairs (see Fig. 45b, 2–1–2), work a whole stitch to join the pairs from the pinhole ground and the workers from the head. From this point, decrease the width gradually by moving the pairs *from* the pinhole ground through the gimp, and, by

1. Pinhole ground
2. Brabant ground
3. Rose ground
4. Cloth and
   Brabant ground
5. Cane ground
6. Tulle
7. Cloth: adding
   and taking off
   extra bobbins
8. Pointed head
9. Half-stitch
   diamond with
   gimp and extra
   pair
10. Picot, working
    both bobbins
11. Gimp in
    pinhole ground
12. Tallies
13. Gimp pair
14. Gimp thread
    close to the
    thread
15. Finishing off
    with a solid
    end

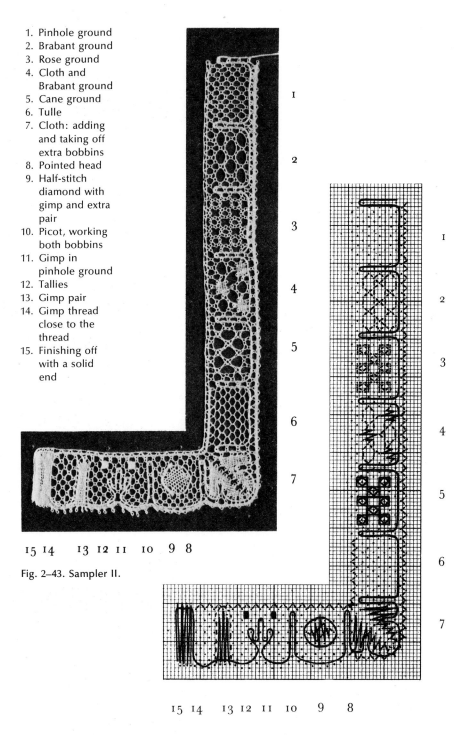

Fig. 2–43. Sampler II.

Fig. 2–44. Pattern for Sampler II.

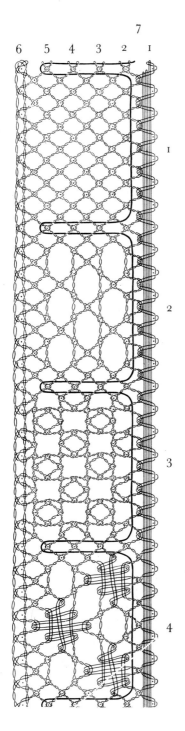

Fig. 2–45a. Hanging the bobbins. Sampler II.

37

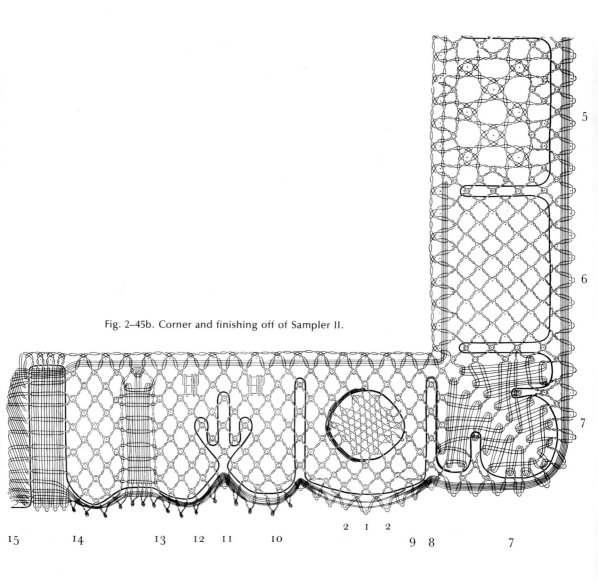

Fig. 2–45b. Corner and finishing off of Sampler II.

5

6

7

2 1 2

15   14   13   12   11   10   9 8   7

whole stitch, through the pairs at the head. Twist the workers and pin-up, then re-join the pairs by whole stitch. (See Fig. 2–45b.)

9. *Half-stitch diamond with gimp and extra pair*. This has already been described in Sampler I. Hang two extra pairs of bobbins on the gimp, twist them, and join them to the ground by half-stitching in the usual way. Work a twist on each side of the gimp when transferring from half-stitch diamond to the pinhole ground. When you are finished with the extra

pairs, tie them together, placing their threads alongside the gimp in opposite directions. Overlap the gimp and continue with the pinhole ground. Cut off the extra pair of gimps when the threads are secure.

10. *Picot with a pair of bobbins.* In working this technique, first twist the workers five times. Before pinning-up (at an angle toward the head), place the pin underneath the outside thread, enclosing it with a twist. The other thread is then lifted and placed round the same pin and both are twisted twice. (See Figs. 2–46a and b.) Join the workers to the head again by whole stitch.

11. *Gimp thread.* When inserting a gimp into the pattern, twist it before and after insertion, even if, as in this case, it passes twice within the same pinhole space.

12. *Tallies.* See Figs. 2–37 and 2–38.

13. *Gimp pair,* identified by whole stitch and twist. The pair in the cloth head nearest to the gimp will pass it, and from now on it is worked with whole stitch and twist according to the pattern shown in Fig. 2–45b.

14. *Gimp thread.* Insert the gimp thread close to the cloth. No twist is required after it is inserted, since the gimp threads are laid in opposite directions to those of the workers in the cloth.

15. *Finishing off the sampler with solid end.* Work a whole stitch. After the last pinning-up on the footside, continue using whole stitch with the workers through three pairs of bobbins, and then lay the workers aside (right across the lace). Twist the next pair once, and work the previous pair through four pairs, using whole stitch. Repeat this progression with succeeding pairs until only three pairs remain. Tie a loop in one of the threads, in order to take it round the other threads and to fold it against the underside. Tie the threads up. Cut off these worked-in threads as close as possible to the lace.

Fig. 2–46 a, b, c. Picot, worked with a pair of bobbins.

Fig. 2–47a. 'Lily of the Valley' designed by Satu Carlsten.
Fig. 47b. 'Dew drops' designed by Sally Johanson.

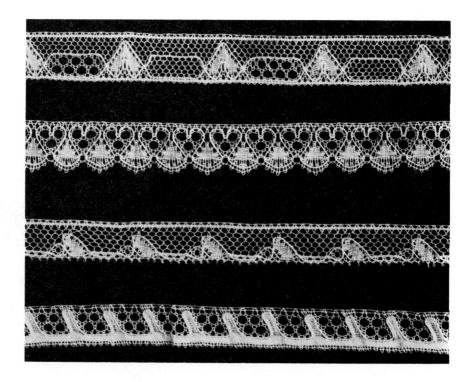

Fig. 2–48a. Bobbin-worked hearts, re-designed from an old pattern. Fig. 2–48b. 'Hearts and fans', an old design. Fig. 2–48c. 'Frogs', re-designed from an old pattern.
Fig. 2–48d. 'Cock's comb'. The last two designs were copied from photographs at the Nordiska Museet, Sweden.

Fig. 2–49. 'Cross triumphant', altar lace designed by Märta Afzelius.

Fig. 2–50. 'Te Deum', altar lace designed by Sten Kauppi. From the Sacristy, Johanneslunds Church, Linköping.

Fig. 2–51. 'Crystals', chalice cloth designed by Märta Afzelius.

41

3. Final stages

This chapter provides supplementary information intended to be helpful in working various lace grounds.

To join edgings, choose a starting-point in the design where the joining is least likely to be conspicuous; in many cases, this would be on the diagonal. There are a number of places in Sampler I to finish off in different grounds. For example, where the clothwork stretches right across the lace, you can start at the point illustrated in Fig. 6–1. Handkerchief edgings are finished best in the middle of a side, where the join shows least. In other techniques, edgings are usually joined at or near a corner.

Finish edgings along the same row as that on which the work was started. Tie the threads together pair by pair with a reef knot, and cut them off. Sew the edgings with a finer thread than that used in the lace, first on the top side, then on the underside.

Lace which starts like the pattern shown in Fig. 2–36, for example, is finished by placing the first set of stitches on top of the corresponding row which completed the work. In general, sewing should be started with the footside; if you begin with the head, make sure that you draw out a long enough thread to allow the underside to be sewn as well. Sew through both parts, using the holes of the pins, and working the stitches round the two portions, in order to ensure a firm and almost invisible join. Stitch twice for every knot to secure the cut threads properly. This kind of stitch sewing is easier if the threads have not been cut off too short. When the edgings are finished, cut the threads off as close to the lace as possible.

Where a lace starts in clothwork as in Fig. 6–1, finish by working a full row of the same pattern, tie together pair by pair with a reef knot, and cut. To join the ends of an edging, lay the beginning of the lace on top, work a few concealed stitches first on the top side, then on the underside, in order to hide the knots between the two cloths.

Another method of joining is to tie each pair of threads together with a half-reef knot which later can be untied. Cut the threads long enough so that the ends are concealed by the pattern when sewn in with a needle.

Footside is usually worked with whole stitch and twist. Where an exceptional distance separates the pins, give an extra twist to the outermost pair, thus providing greater firmness. This will be less necessary where pins lie close together, as in the footside shown in Figs. 6–1—6–4.

Head. When working passives into a head, twist the workers twice, usually when pinning-up at the outer edge. Figs. 6–5 and 6–6 illustrate how to join the ground. When working the cloth as shown in Figs. 6–5 and 6–6, change the workers round at the corner.

If working half-stitch diamond at the head, give an extra twist only to laces worked in fine linen. (See Fig. 6–8.)

Give an extra twist to the pair enclosing a pin when working a whole stitch and twist, as in Figs. 6–9 and 6–10.

In the case of some laces, a closely-woven head may be built up by taking any pair of workers out to the head. Support these workers on pins so that they are included lengthways in the cloth until they are returned from the head. Twist the workers in pinning-up, as in Fig. 6–12.

Likewise, twist the workers and pin-up when a plait passes through the cloth. (See Fig. 6–13.)

Plaits are normally worked with two pairs. (See Fig. 2–33.) Fig. 6–14 shows how to proceed with three pairs, i.e. join the plaits with a whole stitch. Twist the workers only on the outside of the plait. To work four

Fig. 3–1. Christina pillow, patented by Harald Westergren. The lace shown is called 'Vanity', an old pattern re-designed.

pairs under normal conditions, treat each pair as *one* bobbin, and work a series of half-stitches, as in Figs. 2–33 and 6–15.

Picots can also be added to a plait by bringing in a pin from underneath, twisting the thread and fastening it to form a loop. (See Fig. 6–16.) In addition to the method illustrated in Sampler II, picot in cloth can also be worked as shown in Fig. 2–46c.

Clothwork. When two pairs of workers meet at a pinning-up in a cloth, give a twist to the pair that continues as the workers. (See Fig. 6–17.) Make a hole in the cloth by changing the workers round, as in Fig. 6–18; no extra twist is needed.

Special features can be included in certain laces, such as an open head. Figs. 2–19 and 6–19 show how to work this lengthways. Fig. 6–20 shows an open head worked across as follows: (a.) twist threads once or several times, as the pattern moves lengthways, (b.) work whole stitch with double pairs, (c.) twist and half-stitch, (d.) twist, and whole stitch and twist.

When a square figure is situated as in Figs. 6–21 and 6–22, the two pairs to be added simultaneously at 'x' should previously have been worked in by using the same stitch as in the ground. Likewise, the two pairs at 'o' should be joined before they enter the surrounding ground.

To produce a more closely woven, denser cloth such as some lace requires, more bobbins can be brought in than are shown in the pattern for the intervening ground. However, do not worry about how to take out the extra pairs belonging to a pattern figure within a cloth; they can be moved around in a number of ways, e.g. two pairs, joined by several half-stitches, can pass through torchon, as in Fig. 6–23. An extra pair can be shared with a gimp, provided that it also shares its general direction. (See Fig. 6–24.) The pinning-up of two pairs that are to be taken out of a ground simultaneously can be accomplished as shown in Fig. 6–25. To bring an extra pair of bobbins in to the cloth, follow the same procedure as in the pinning-up illustrated in Figs. 6–26 and 6–33.

Take out extra pairs of bobbins as shown in Fig. 6–27. Tie the threads together with a half-reef knot, laying them alongside the nearest thread, one in each direction.

If a gimp must pass twice between two adjacent rows (particularly in coarse laces), do not twist any of the pairs until both gimp threads have passed through. At the pin where the gimp turns back on its path, twist the pair closest to the catch pin, as in Fig. 6–28.

Similarly, a gimp may be retained if the bobbins of the nearest pair change places after passing the gimp, i.e. if they alter the shed. Alternatively, twist the pair before it returns to its starting point, as illustrated in Figs. 6–7 and 6–29.

When a gimp passes through the cloth, make sure that there is always a twist to separate the gimp from the cloth threads. (Figs. 6–11 and 6–30.)

If there is a row of pins at the corner of a lace, the whole corner should

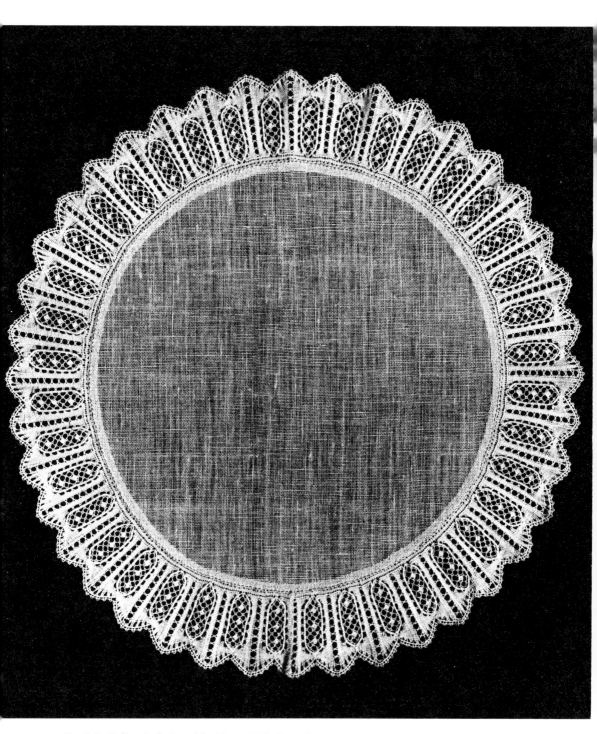

Fig. 3–2. 'Foliage', designed by Nanna Willy Danielsson.

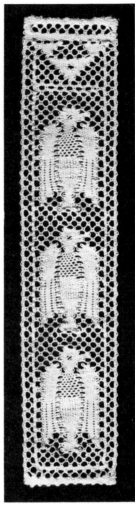

Fig. 3–4. 'Johannes eagle', bookmark designed by Märta Afzelius.

Fig. 3–3a. 'Crown', from Anna Lovisa Hartwick's pattern book. Östergötlands Museum, Sweden. Fig. 3–3b. 'Funnel', designed by Olle Danielsson. Fig. 3–3c. 'Ermine', designed by Sten Kauppi.

be turned a quarter turn, and the pair of bobbins being worked from the foot toward the head should be returned to its place at the foot. If the pair is unable to follow the gimp (Fig. 6–24), take it out of the head as inconspicuously as possible, and add it to the foot, as in Fig. 6–31. This diagram also illustrates how to use two extra pairs in the corner of a cloth. Note that the threads are to be divided so that one bobbin is added from each pair in the cloth. When the corner has been turned, add the corresponding bobbins to the cloth as a single pair. Subsequently, take out two more pairs.

An additional feature can be added to some grounds, e.g. Dieppe, by working one or several pairs of bobbins in half-stitch or whole stitch, as detailed in Figs. 6–36 and 6–37, and incorporated in the laces shown on pp. 46, 51, and 59.

To make a tulle ground firmer, work in more twists than are set out in Sampler II.

To work corners in tulle ground, add and take out pairs of bobbins, as illustrated in Fig. 6–34.

Fig. 3–5. 'Catch of fish', designed by Märta Afzelius.

a.   d.   c.

b.   e.

f.

Fig. 3–6a, b, c. Bellman lace, revision of an old design, shown in three mounting variations. Fig. 3–6d. 'Midsummer garland', designed by Satu Carlsten. Fig. 3–6e. 'Mussels', designed by Satu Carlsten. Fig. 3–6f. 'Wedges', designed by Sten Kauppi.

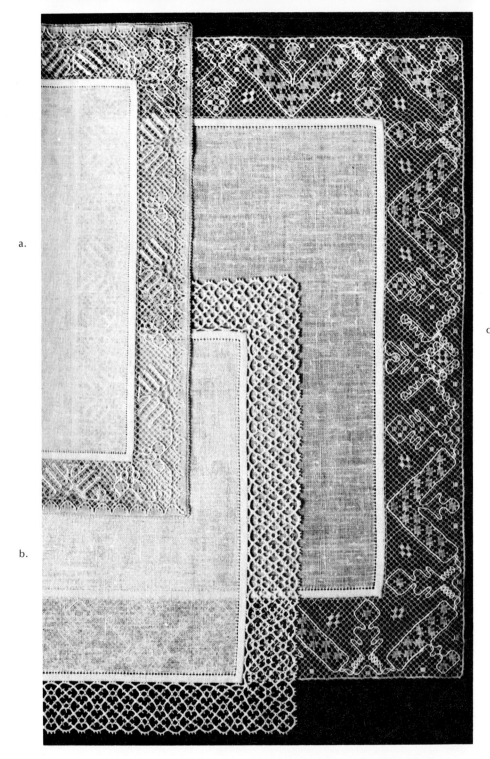

a.

c.

b.

Fig. 3–7a. 'Sunlit waves', an old design. Fig. 3–7b. Kumla lattice, after the original in gold and silver. Kumla Church, 1642. (Photo by ATA.) Fig. 3–7c. Tuna lace, after the original in gold, early 18th century. (Photo by ATA.)

4. Mounting lace

The mounting of bobbin-made lace should be confined to linen articles (with the possible exception of sheets).

The linen of the article should match the lace in question. In addition, consider the article in relation to the design, density, and thread thickness of the lace. For table mats and other small articles, the density (closeness) of the linen should harmonize with that of the lace's ground.

Fine linen is suitable for fine handkerchief lace; linen for altar cloths and other large articles should also be of a close and firm weave. Give consideration in mounting to both the width of the hem and the manner of sewing. Remember to keep a narrow hem facing the lace. An example of a handwoven linen finished with a narrow hem is illustrated in Fig. 2–51.

The hem is stitched by pulling out a thread and, with a lace linen thread, stitching round three threads.

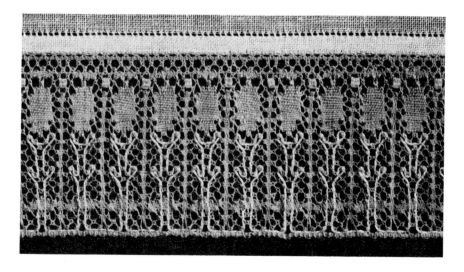

Fig. 4–1. 'Rising smoke', designed by Satu Carlsten.

Fig. 4–2. 'Eyebright', a christening robe and christening cushion designed by
Hilda Starck-Lilienberg.

Use embroidery sparingly on table mats and table cloths already
trimmed with lace. If it is applied, it must not be so conspicuous
that it eclipses the lace, which should be the principal embellishment.
On the other hand, a simple, stiff embroidery might be appropriate in
certain circumstances, if it emphasizes the beauty of the lace.

The ends of a lace which is to be inserted into a piece of material or
an altar cloth can be finished off by working a separate strip, for which
special patterns are available. (See the illustration on p. 54.) In this
method of mounting, fold the end of the main lace and sew the strip to
the underside, or, in some cases, bend the strip round the end of the
main piece before sewing on.

A lace that is mounted on bed linen should have a compact and firm
texture, and should be strong enough to withstand constant washing. In
these circumstances, a narrow lace is usually preferable to a broad one.

To attach lace on to a sheet in the traditional manner, the width of the end piece should be 2–3 in. (50–80 mm.); the top hem of the other piece should be ⅕–⅓ in. (5–8 mm.). After folding the end piece, machine-sew the hem and turn it inside-out. Sew the lace on to this hem, holding it tight against the machine-stitches and between the two hem surfaces. Then extract one or two threads, and hem-stitch the lace on to the narrow hem of the other piece. To strengthen the lace, which is strongly recommended, sew a piece of linen tape on to both ends, as described above.

Sew on lace rather loosely, since it will shrink more than the material on

Fig. 4–3. 'Palm Sunday', designed and executed by Greta Sandberg.

Fig. 4–4. 'Flowering shrub', designed by Nanna Willy Danielsson.

which it is attached. Allow about 5% shrinkage for medium and fine lace, and about 5 to 10% for coarse lace.

Lace intended for mounting on large pieces of material must be pre-shrunk. This is done as follows: place the lace on a soft ironing board, cover with a thin, wet cloth, and very lightly apply a hot iron. The steam will shrink the lace. Repeat a few times and lay the lace flat to dry. Altar lace may be treated in the same way.

To sew lace on to handkerchiefs, remove a thread before tacking on the lace. Turn the edge of the material and stitch from the footside through the double material, thus strengthening the join. When completed, cut off any excess material on the underside, close to the seam. Sew with a soft, mercerized thread.

Lace can be mounted on a circular piece of material in a similar fashion. Tack the lace on to the material, and fold the latter as you sew. Sew through the footside as well as the folded material. When completed, cut off any excess material from the underside, close to the seam.

Pages 45 and 48 show another method of mounting lace on a circular cloth. Mark out a circle in the material and tack the lace loosely enough to allow for the rounded shape of the final result.

Hem-stitch the lace. Cut the material on the underside wide enough to

Fig. 4–5. 'Wings', designed by Nanna Willy Danielsson.

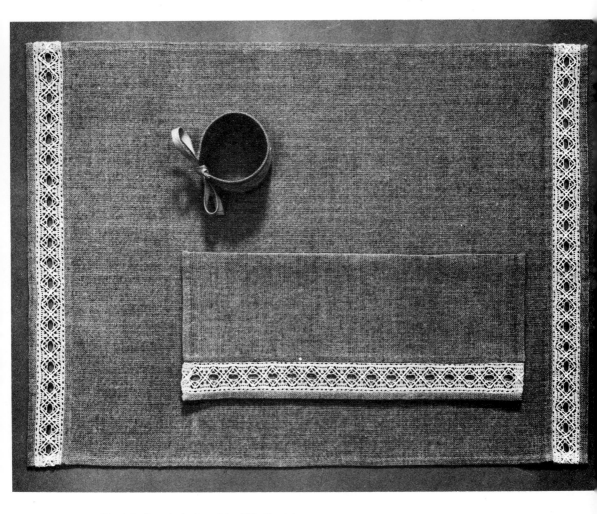

Fig. 4–6. 'I spy', designed by Olle Danielsson.

allow for a hem. Turn the hem and sew with an open button-hole stitch or a slip stitch. The open button-hole stitch is preferable for coarse and open-weave material, and when stitch traces on the right side must be avoided.

When ironing, never touch the lace, only the material. If the lace seems too loose, shrink it by the steam treatment detailed above.

Fig. 4–7. 'Prowling cat', designed by Barbro Wallander.

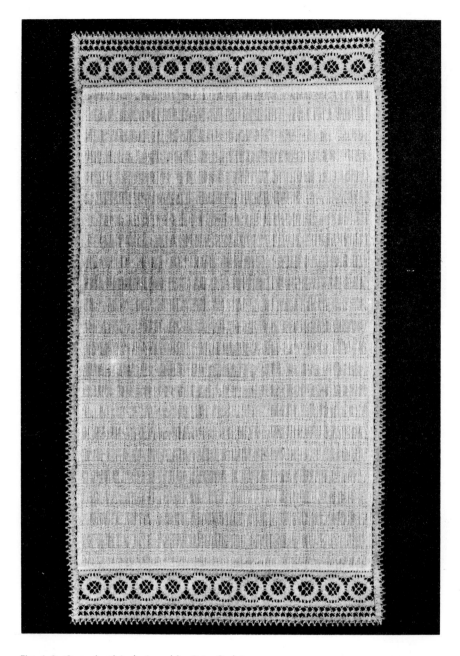

Fig. 4–8. 'Sun wheels', designed by Satu Carlsten.

Fig. 4–9. 'Beehive', designed by Satu Carlsten.

5. Washing instructions

Lace should not be washed unless unavoidable. If washing is necessary, take the overall measurements of the material beforehand. Soak it for a while, first in cold water, then in tepid, soapy water. Squeeze it gently (never rub), and rinse carefully several times. Wrap the article in a towel, and lay it while still damp on a firm, flat surface (such as 'Formica'), covering the surface first with felt, then with a layer of suitable material. Unmounted lace should be rolled round a bottle and left to dry.

Lace-decorated table cloths should be spread out, then pinned down with stainless steel pins, which are left in until the article has dried. Start pinning down from one of the corners, according to the measurements previously noted.

If necessary, lightly iron the article inside-out, and protected by a layer of another material.

Lampshades decorated with lace should be dipped in tepid, soapy water, thoroughly rinsed, preferably under a shower, shaken, and left to dry.

Fig. 5–1. 'Sailboat', designed by Olle Danielsson.

6. Diagrams

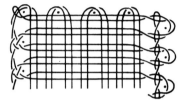

Fig. 6–1. Foot with two pairs of bobbins.

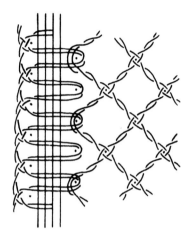

Fig. 6–2. Foot with three pairs
of bobbins.

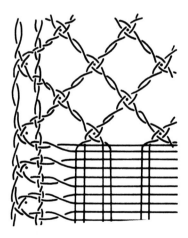

Fig. 6–3. Foot with two pairs of bobbins.

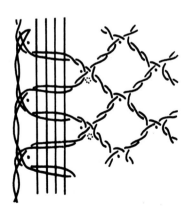

Fig. 6–4. Foot with two pairs
of bobbins.

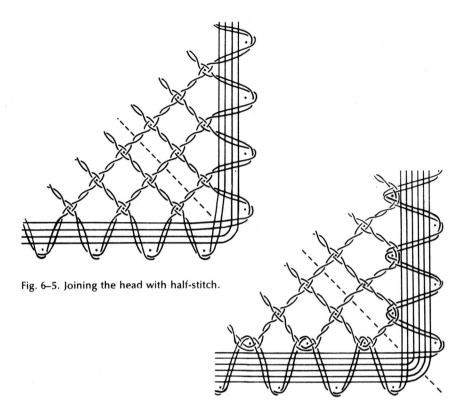

Fig. 6–5. Joining the head with half-stitch.

Fig. 6–6. Joining the head with whole stitch.

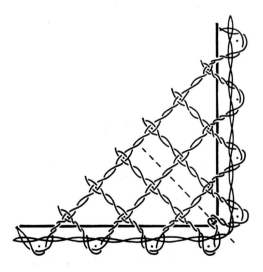

Fig. 6–7. Securing the gimp.

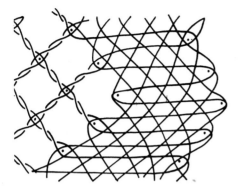

Fig. 6–8. Head with half-stitch diamond.

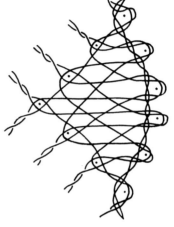

Fig. 6–9. Half-stitch diamond with whole stitch and twist at edge.

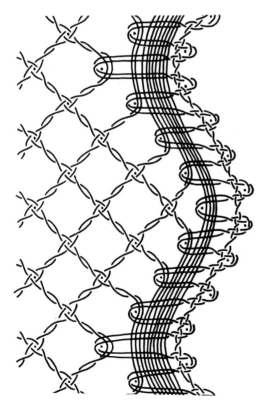

Fig. 6–10. Head with clothwork and whole stitch and twist at edge.

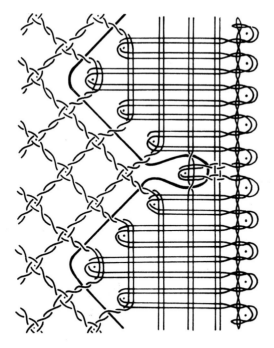

Fig. 6–11. Insertion of the gimp into clothwork.

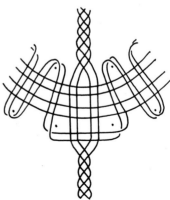

Fig. 6–13. Plait passing through clothwork.

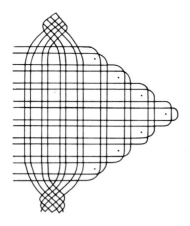

Fig. 6–12. Workers supported by pins in order to extend the head.

Fig. 6–14. Plait worked from three pairs of bobbins.

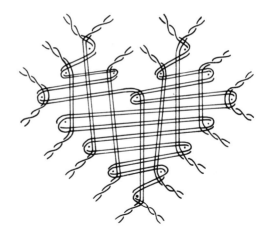

Fig. 6–17. Two workers meeting at a pinning-up in the cloth.

Fig. 6–15. Plaits joined to form a double plait.

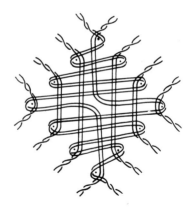

Fig. 6–18. Forming a hole in the cloth.

Fig. 6–16. Plaits with picots.

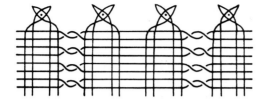

Fig. 6–19. Open head, lengthways.

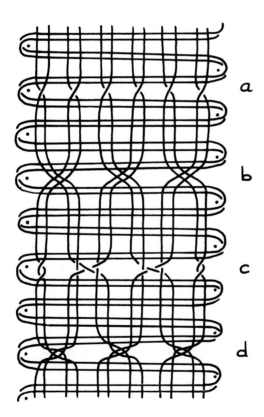

a

b

c

d

Fig. 6–20. Open head, across.

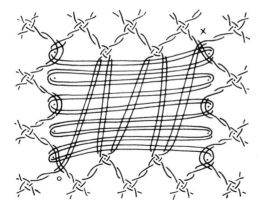

Fig. 6–21. Cloth square with two pairs
of bobbins joined without pinning-up.

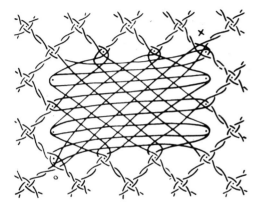

Fig. 6–22. Half-stitch diamond square
with two pairs of bobbins joined
without pinning-up.

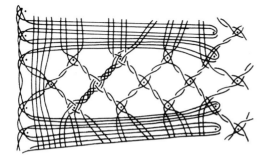

Fig. 6–23. Introducing an extra pair of
bobbins by forming a plait with another
pair.

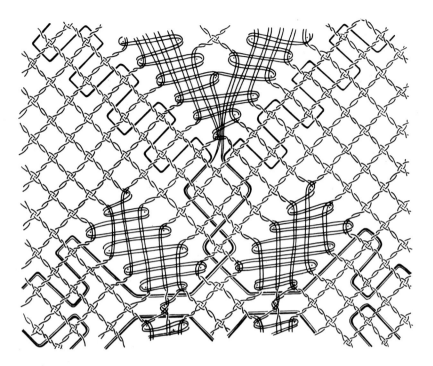

Fig. 6–24. An extra pair of bobbins following the same pattern as the gimp.

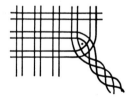

Fig. 6–25. Two pairs of bobbins removed from the cloth simultaneously.

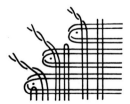

Fig. 6–26. Adding an extra pair of bobbins to the cloth.

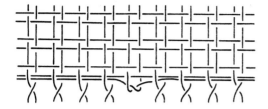

Fig. 6–27. Taking out an extra pair of bobbins from the cloth.

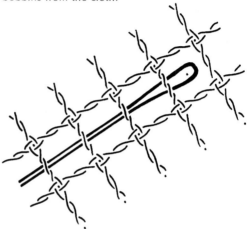

Fig. 6–28. Gimp turning round a catch pin.

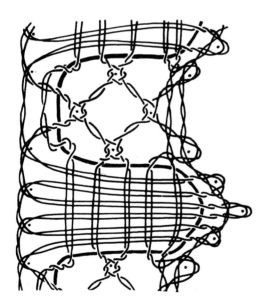

Fig. 6–29. Gimp enclosing the cloth and keeping it in position.

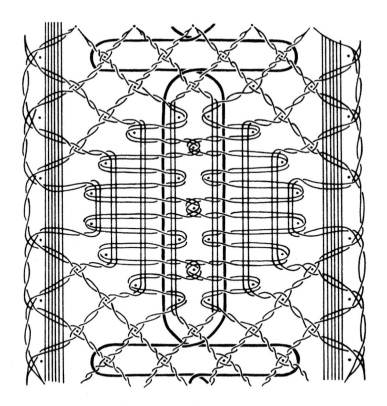

Fig. 6–30. Gimp inserted in to the cloth.

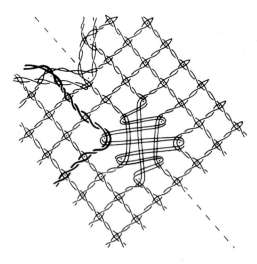

Fig. 6–31. Row of pins at the corner. Two extra pairs of bobbins must be inserted.

Fig. 6–32. Two gimp threads change place.

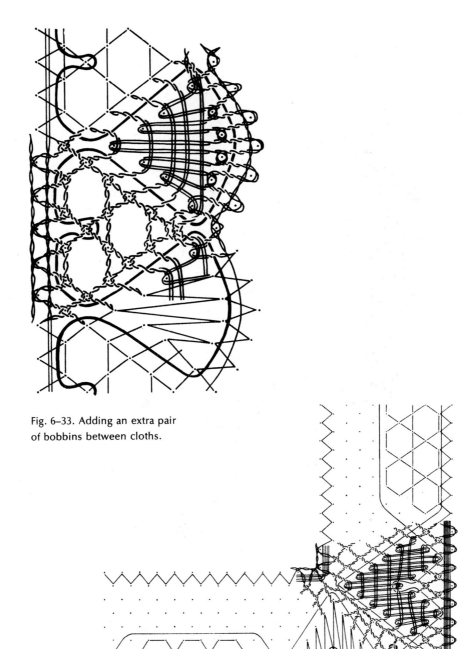

Fig. 6–33. Adding an extra pair
of bobbins between cloths.

Fig. 6–34. Corner with tulle ground; an extra pair of bobbins is added.

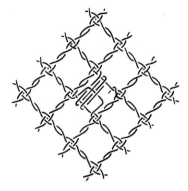

Fig. 6–35. Dieppe ground with a tally.

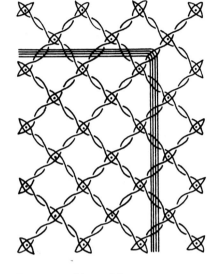

Fig. 6–37. Additional feature worked by whole stitch through a Dieppe ground.

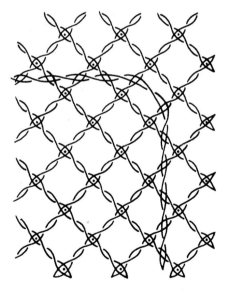

Fig. 6–36. Additional feature worked by whole stitch and twist through a Dieppe ground.

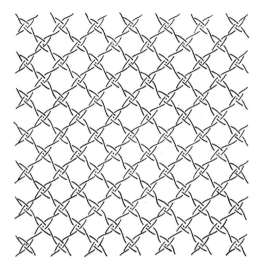

Fig. 6–38. Torchon ground.

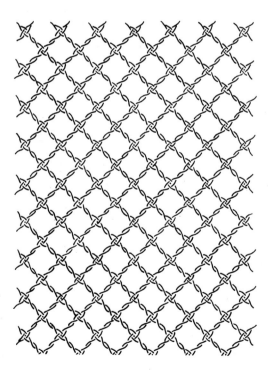

Fig. 6–39. Dieppe ground.

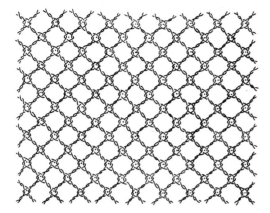

Fig. 6–40. Pinhole ground.

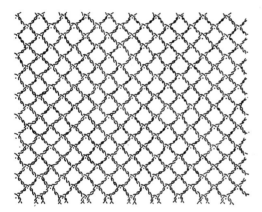

Fig. 6–41. Tulle ground.

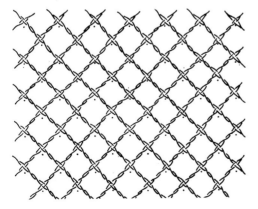

Fig. 6–42. Whole stitch ground.

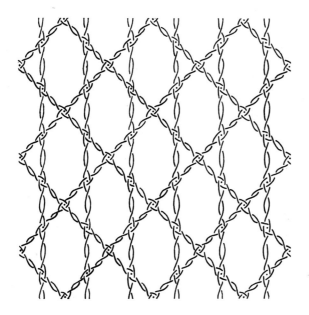

Fig. 6–43. Brabant ground.

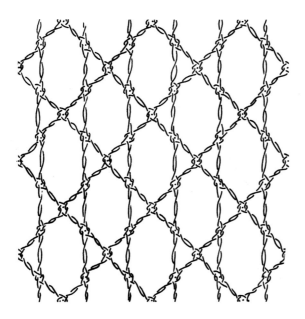

Fig. 6–44. Brabant ground.

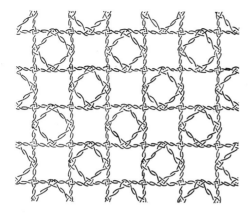

Fig. 6–45. Rose ground.

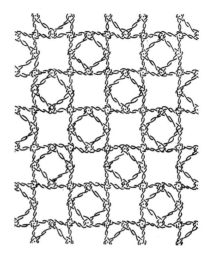

Fig. 6–47. Rose ground.

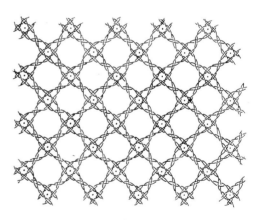

Fig. 6–48. Cane ground.

Fig. 6–46. Rose ground.

7. Details of materials

Page	Name and width of lace	Thread No. of bobbins	Quality of linen*	Thread for mounting	Width of hem	Stitch	Fig. No
4	The King's lace Bridal crown of gold thread height 92 mm.						
6	St. Lars lace 53 mm.	Eng. linen 50/2 35 pairs bobbins 18/5 1 pair bobbins					6–24
40	'Lily of the Valley' 18 mm.	Eng. linen 2002/2 18 pairs bobbins LC 25 1 pair bobbins	m 39 × 35 thread	DMC No. 30 or 25 thread		Close overcast	
40	'Dew drops' 9 mm.	Eng. linen 160/2 18 pairs bobbins LC 25 1	m 39 × 35 thread		4 mm.; at tape 7 mm.	For hem, hem-stitch with drawn thread	6–29
40	'Bobbin-worked hearts' 15 mm.	Eng. linen 200/2 16 pairs bobbins LC 25 + 1 thread 200/2 1 pair bobbins					6–34
40	'Hearts and fans' 15 mm.	Eng. linen 200/2 12 pairs bobbins LC 25 1 bobbin					6–33
40	'Frogs' 13 mm.	Eng. linen 160/2 13 pairs bobbins LC 25 1 pair bobbins					2–46

* m = machine-made, h = hand-made. Numbers = threads/cm.², warp – weft.

Page	Name and width of lace	Thread No. of bobbins	Quality of linen*	Thread for mounting	Width of hem	Stitch	Fig. No.
40	'Cock's comb' 12 mm.	Eng. linen 180/2 or 160/2 15 pairs bobbins LC 25 1 bobbin					
41	'Cross triumphant' 102 mm.	Eng. linen 20/3					
41	'Te Deum' 93 mm.						
41	'Crystals' 26 mm.						
43	'Vanity' 78 mm.	Eng. linen 160/2 64 pairs bobbins 3 bobbins with 4 threads 160/2					
45	'Foliage' 45 mm. cloth 31 cm. dia.	Eng. linen 60/2 26 pairs bobbins 18/3 1 pair	h 14 × 14 thread	80/2–90/2	5 mm.	Hem-stitch with drawn thread slip stitch	
46	'Crown' 39 mm.	Eng. linen 40/2 17 pairs bobbins	m 15 × 15 thread	70/2	3 mm.	Straight satin stitch	6–13
46	'Funnel' 28 mm.	Eng. linen 80/2 21 pairs bobbins 18/3 1 bobbin	m 18 × 18 thread	90/2–100/2	4 mm.	Hem-stitch with drawn thread	
46	'Ermine' 23 mm.	Eng. linen 50/2 14 pairs bobbins	m 14 × 14 thread	80/2–90/2	5 mm.	Hem-stitch with drawn thread	
46	'Johannes eagle' 40 mm.	Eng. linen 50/2 31 pairs bobbins					6–27 6–37

* m = machine-made, h = hand-made. Numbers = threads/cm.², warp – weft.

Page	Name and width of lace	Thread No. of bobbins	Quality of linen*	Thread for mounting	Width of hem	Stitch	Fig. No.
47	'Catch of fish' 50 mm.						
48	Bellman lace 25 mm.	Eng. linen 20/3 8 pairs bobbins	h 9 × 8 thread	70/2–80/2	5 mm.	Hem with open button-hole stitch. Short ends of runner hem-stitch with drawn thread. Work slip stitch for sewing on lace. Hem-stitch with drawn thread worked for the round table cloth	
48	'Midsummer garland' 63 mm.	Eng. linen 20/3 25 pairs bobbins					
48	'Mussels' 29 mm.	Eng. linen 50/3 18 pairs bobbins 18/5 1 pair bobbins	h 9 × 8 thread	70/2–80/2	5 mm.	Hem with open button-hole stitch, double-folded edge of material joined to lace by overstitch. For finishing off, see p. 54, underside, head, and foot	6–30
49	'Wedges' 51 mm.	Eng. linen 20/3 18 pairs bobbins	h 9 × 8 thread	70/2–80/2	5 mm.	Open button-hole stitch	
50	'Sunlit waves' 38 mm.	Eng. linen 80/2 22 pairs bobbins 18/3 2 pairs bobbins	m 18 × 18 thread	90/2–100/2	5 mm.	Hem-stitch with drawn thread	6–11 6–28
50	Kumla lattice 37 mm.	Eng. linen 40/3 16 pairs bobbins +2 pairs extra for corners	m 14 × 14 thread	70/2–80/2	5 mm.	Hem-stitch with drawn thread	2–33 6–16
50	Tuna lace 54 mm.	Eng. linen 50/2 or Eng. linen 60/2 31 pairs bobbins 18/5 1 pair bobbins	m 14 × 14 thread	80/2	5 mm.	Hem-stitch with drawn thread	6–5 6–32 6–35

* m = machine-made, h = hand-made. Numbers = threads/cm.², warp – weft.

age	Name and width of lace	Thread No. of bobbins	Quality of linen*	Thread for mounting	Width of hem	Stitch	Fig. No.
1	'Rising smoke' 47 mm.	Eng. linen 120/2 40 pairs + 1 pair extra at corner LC 25 1 bobbin	m 18 × 18 thread	90/2–100/2	4 mm.	Hem-stitch with drawn thread	6–21 6–36
2	'Eyebright' 10 mm. (Christening robe)	Eng. linen 120/2 10 pairs bobbins	m 39 × 35 thread	80/2	3 mm. at lace 10 mm. below	Machine. Hemming-up	2–33
2	For collar and sleeves Head & foot 4 mm.	Eng. linen 120/2 5 pairs bobbins	m 39 × 35 thread	160/2	4 mm. at lace 7 mm. at tape hem	Hem-stitch with drawn thread. Hemming-up.	
4	'Flowering shrub' 42 mm.	Eng. linen 50/2 27 pairs bobbins 18/5 1 bobbin	h 15 × 15 thread	80/2–90/2	5 mm.	Hem-stitch with drawn thread	6–28
5	'Wings' 13 mm.	Eng. linen 90/2 14 pairs bobbins	m 39 × 35 thread	140/2–160/2	3 mm.	Hemming-up	
6	'I spy' 20 mm.	Eng. linen 50/3 12 pairs bobbins	m 13 × 13 thread	80/2–90/2	5 mm.	Slip stitch. Sew lace by overstitch to mat & napkin bag, folding edge of material double. Sew on lace working overstitch, fold material and hem-up; finish off with ribbon for napkin ring	2–28 2–29 2–36
7	'Prowling cat' 26 mm. At upper edge of shade 5 mm. Height of lamp 23·7 cm.	Eng. linen 50/2 18 pairs bobbins Eng. linen 50/2 5 pairs bobbins	m 15 × 15 thread	80/2			
8	'Sun wheels' 51 mm. lace running lengthwise 11 mm., worked in one piece.	Eng. linen 50/3 27 pairs bobbins 6 pairs bobbins	h 16 × 16 thread	80/2–90/2	5 mm.	Slip stitch	6–35
9	'Beehive' 19 mm.	Eng. linen 80/2 16 pairs bobbins 18/3 1 bobbin	m 15 × 15 thread	for hem-stitch with drawn thread and four-sided stitch 90/2; for embroidery 50/3	4 mm.	Hem-stitch with drawn thread and four-sided stitch	6–36
0	'Sailboat' 50 mm.	Eng. linen 50/2 31 pairs bobbins 18/5 3 bobbins				Straight satin stitch	

m = machine-made, h = hand-made. Numbers = threads/cm.², warp – weft.

Suppliers

Great Britain

Mace & Nairn, 89 Crane St., Salisbury, Wilts., SP1 2PY
sell bobbins, and linen yarn.

The Needlewoman Shop, 146 Regent St., London W.1
sell bobbins, and cotton and linen yarn.

Christine Riley, 53 Barclay St., Stonehaven, Kincardineshire, AB3 2AR
sell bobbins, and cotton yarn.

No manufacturer or importer of lace pillows in Great Britain can at present be traced. It is hoped that this situation will soon be remedied, but in the meantime readers are recommended to make their own pillows. The Swedish Lace-Making Association will provide any equipment not otherwise available. Their address is: Föreningen Svenska Spetsar, Box 2022, S-580 02, Lipköping 2, Sweden.

United States

Some Place, 2990 Adeline St., Berkeley, Calif. 94703
sell a basic bobbin lace kit.

Berga/Ullman, Box 831, Ossining, New York, N.Y. 10562
sell a traditional Swedish padded lace pillow, bobbins etc.

Yarn Center, 866 Avenue of the Americas, New York, N.Y.
sell a wide variety of yarns.

Robin and Russ Handweavers, 533 North Adams Street, McMinniville, Oregon 97128 sell a wide variety of yarns.

Merribee Needlecraft Company, 2904 West Lancaster, Fort Worth, Texas 76107 sell yarns by mail order, also have a number of retail shops.

Frederick J. Fawcett, Inc., 129 South Street, Boston, Mass. 02111
sell all kinds of linen yarn.

Index of working diagrams